HIDDEN HANDS

All royalties from this book will go towards
the work of CAFOD amongst under-privileged
children in the Third World.

HIDDEN HANDS

*Child Workers
Around the World*

EDITED BY
Peter Stanford

FOREWORD BY
Rachel Billington

Collins
FOUNT PAPERBACKS

First published in Great Britain by Fount paperbacks,
London in 1988

Copyright in the Foreword © Rachel Billington 1988
Copyright in the poems © *The Catholic Herald*
and CAFOD 1988
Copyright in the remaining text and in this collection
© Peter Stanford 1988

Printed and bound in Great Britain by
William Collins Sons & Co. Ltd, Glasgow

Conditions of Sale

This book is sold subject to the condition
that it shall not, by way of trade or otherwise,
be lent, re-sold, hired out or otherwise circulated
without the publisher's prior consent in any form of
binding or cover other than that in which it is
published and without a similar condition
including this condition being imposed
on the subsequent purchaser

Contents

Foreword *by Rachel Billington*	1
Preface	3
Kamau's Story	11
Otami's Story	35
Andrelina's Story	59
Child Labour, *by Joanna Moorhead*	83
Bibliography	117

Foreword

Children write good poetry. Even so, it was a daring idea to ask children from the age of four upwards to compose poetry about destitute and misused children living in an alien culture, about whom they previously knew nothing. It might have been a dull exercise, done in a spirit of obedience instead of inspiration. Inspiration was what we hoped for. We did not expect technical accomplishment, although that was a bonus where it came, but we wanted the writers to be inspired by the stories of the three unfortunate children, and to sympathise with their predicament. Only then could our Western children, well-fed and well-educated, hope to write worthwhile poetry.

In the event, the most notable characteristic of the entries we received was the emotion that came through even the simplest of lines – or perhaps, best of all through the simplest of lines.

> *If I was that child*
> *I would be frightened.*
> *If I was that child*
> *I would be crying...*

This was the opening to one of our prize-winners'

poems. To their authors' total credit, the poems, prize-winning or not, proved that our children's imaginations have not yet been deadened by the modern continuous news coverage of death and destruction round the world. They can still be moved by the plight of an individual like Kamau or Andrelina. Indeed, in an era of anonymous poverty as pictured on television or in the newspapers, we felt that it was the very individualizing of poverty and ill-treatment that was most helpful to our entrants. They had to put themselves in the place of one child with a particular set of problems.

We judges had to separate eight poems from the rest, to be read out in the Royal Festival Hall. We watched these talented children arrive escorted by their proud and caring parents. It was a moving experience to see such healthy, well-turned out and, as it happened, good-looking children, reading out their thoughts about their destitute contemporaries. The physical appearance of privilege made the contrast in the situation between the reader and the subject of his poem real and poignant. Even more important, their voices spoke with the sort of directness that few adults could achieve. We would like to have chosen eighty to read instead of only eight.

Now this book, skilfully edited by Peter Stanford, gives a wider sample of the poems and also sets them in context. There is a lot of information here and a lot of passion. Child poverty and child abuse is news. But the child worker is almost forgotten. I feel honoured to have been part of an attempt to remedy this situation, and full of admiration for our child poets.

Rachel Billington

Preface

For every labour there is a reason, and a child for every labour under heaven:

> A child to hoist, and a child to tow;
> A child to hire out, and a child to lock in;
> A child to reap, and a child to sew;
> A child to push, and a child to pull.
> What gain has the child from his toil?

Newsweek, January 1983

In 1987 CAFOD – the Catholic Fund for Overseas Development – celebrated the Silver Jubilee of its work on behalf of the people in need in the Third World. CAFOD's has been a two part task.

Firstly, to educate people in the West about the realities of the developing world. "They" have tried for twenty-five years to explain to "us" why it is that the bulk of the world's people go to bed hungry every night, while a small, privileged group in the developed countries squanders food; why the people of the Third World walk miles to collect drinking water that we wouldn't think fit for a sewer; and why their children miss out on a childhood as we would understand it, instead shouldering an adult's burdens as young as five or six.

The second aim of CAFOD has been to bring development, independence, and, in their wake, justice to the peoples of the Third World.

In attempting to reflect the scope of this work, CAFOD and the *Catholic Herald*, one of Britain's leading religious weeklies, decided to mark the jubilee by inviting children in Britain, aged up to sixteen, to study the case of three child labourers – Andrelina, a little Brazilian girl working on a sugar plantation; Otami, who makes clothes in a Thai sweatshop; and Kamau, a fifteen-year-old boy in Nairobi, who survives by cleaning windscreens – and then try to reflect the hopes and fears of those exploited children in the form of verse.

Well over a thousand children across the age range took up the challenge. Their submissions, which make up much of the text of this book, were read by a panel of judges chaired by the distinguished author, Lady Rachel Billington, and consisting of: Frank Field, MP, a former director of the Child Poverty Action Group; critic and author Isabel Quigly; Ken Madine of CAFOD; Peter Osuji, a Nigerian training for the priesthood; and myself on behalf of the *Catholic Herald*.

Eventually eight poems were chosen by the judges. These would be read out by their authors at a gala day to celebrate CAFOD's jubilee at the Royal Festival Hall on 13th June 1987, in the presence of Cardinal Basil Hume, who congratulated each of the writers. However, the judges were so moved and impressed by the hundreds of poems that could not be heard on that occasion that it was decided to put together this collection of them so as to reach a wider audience.

Preface

The entries printed in this book are the result of work done either by individuals working alone, or else as part of classroom activities in the following schools:

All Saints School, York; Birkenhead High School for Girls; Bishop Challoner School, Basingstoke; Blessed Edmund Jones High School, Rhyl; Newlands School, Cleveland; Notre Dame School, Sheffield; Our Lady and All Saints School, Parbold; Sacred Heart School, Redcar; St Andrew's Primary School, Streatham; St Anne's School, Southampton; St Bernadette's School, Kenton; St Charles' School, London W10; St David's School, Mold; St George's High School, Manchester; St Joseph's Convent, Haunton; St Lewis' Primary School, Warrington; St Marie's School, Sheffield; St Martha's Convent, Barnet; St Mary's College, Colwyn Bay; St Mary's Parish, Louth; St Michael's School, Treforest; St William of York School, London SE23; and Woldingham School, Surrey.

I would like to express my thanks and appreciation to the Anti-Slavery Society and their press officer, Alan Whittaker, to June Jackson and Belinda Coote of Oxfam, to Gill Wilcox of UNICEF, and to the staffs of the *Catholic Herald* and CAFOD for their help in putting together this collection. Also to Rachel Billington, Isabel Quigly, Terence Sheehy, Virginia Mitchell, Caroline Willson, and Sarah Baird-Smith of Collins for their patience and encouragement. And finally to Joanna Moorhead, without whose invaluable assistance this collection would have remained uncollected.

The illustrations are the work of Ruth MacDonald and the pupils of Birkenhead High School for Girls Preparatory Department, and of Christine Rosenthal and her pupils at South Wirral High School, Eastham, Merseyside. The Third World photographs have been generously given by UNICEF. Photographs of the prize winners are by Carlos Reyes of the Andes Press Agency.

Peter Stanford

Preface 7

The winners of the Poetry Competition with Peter Stanford, Rachel Billington and Ken Madine.

8 *Hidden Hands*

Lucy Carroll

Cardinal Hume with Polly Rance

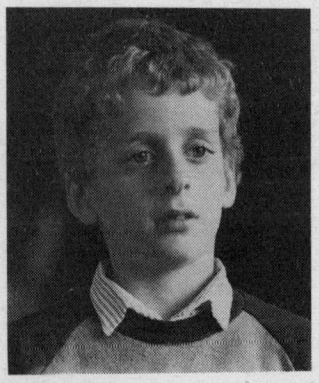

Aidan Turner

Francesca Collins

Preface

Ruth Lythe with Basil Hume

Sarah Hicks

Kyle Tebbitt

Ashley Parr

Kamau's Story

Today we see the frightening spectre of young people who are abandoned or forced into the market-place. We find children and young people in shanty towns and in large impersonal cities where they find meagre sustenance and little or no hope for the future.

Pope John Paul II
World Peace Day 1987

Even the dustbins of Nairobi are stuffed with money, they told Kamau as he set off for the Kenyan capital. The arrival of a seventh baby had made life impossible for his family. They had little money to feed an extra mouth, and not enough room in their home. The meagre living they made from farming could no longer support them all. So Kamau, at fifteen the eldest child, was told that it was time for him to make his own way in the world.

With a mixture of sadness at leaving behind all that he knew, fear at the new life which lay ahead, and excitement at being free and independent, Kamau leapt aboard a train bound for Nairobi, clinging to the roof throughout the long journey.

Hidden Hands

Like the rest of the estimated one in three children in the Third World who inhabit the cities and their slums, Kamau did not find the streets paved with gold. The most that the dustbins yielded were a few scraps of food, or other people's rubbish which he then tried to sell for coppers.

However, Kamau was lucky and found a friend in Njoroge, who had grown up in the city and therefore knew how to survive its hardships. Together the two fifteen-year-olds would stand at the main road junctions. When there was a rush of traffic they would run out and offer to wash the windows of a passing car. With Njoroge's coaching, Kamau grew skilled and agile at darting in and out of the moving vehicles in search of a customer.

Kamau's Story

They would work day and night until they made enough to eat. Sometimes, after dark, they would peer through the windows they were cleaning and see rich businessmen or foreign tourists on their way to the smart bars and cafes of Nairobi for the evening.

Dressed in rags and with scarcely enough to eat, Kamau and Njoroge could not even begin to imagine what such places were like. All they had to look forward to was a dirty shop doorway, or a park bench, where they would try to sleep amid the constant bustle of this overcrowded city.

But then one day Njoroge was not quick enough. As he rushed towards a customer, another car came racing down the outside lane and knocked him down. It drove off without even so much as a backward glance from its driver.

Kamau was now on his own. He grew frightened. Would he meet the same fate as Njoroge? And if he was to fall under the wheels of a passing car or lorry, who would spare him a second thought now that Njoroge was dead?

Kamau sank into a deep depression. He began to dream of the family he had left behind, so many miles from Nairobi, amid the peace and safety of the countryside. Did they still think of him, he wondered?

Kamau was faced with two choices – to go back home or to stay in the city. But he didn't know what kind of welcome would greet him at home. Hadn't they told him to go and make his own way in the world? And then would he want to be treated as a child again, now that he had sampled the independence of a street child's life?

But if he remained in Nairobi, he couldn't last on his own. He had often seen the gangs of other street children roaming around. Perhaps he could join in with one of these?

Njoroge had warned him though that these gangs made a living by picking pockets and stealing. Kamau had never taken anything that was not his own, or that had not been abandoned in a dustbin. Yet as he observed these street gangs and the way they preyed on the bags of foreign tourists in particular, he knew that he was agile enough to do the same.

For many of the street children who, like Kamau, come to inhabit the big cities of the Third World and their back alleys, crime is a way of life, of living. Right and wrong are rapidly forgotten in the battle to survive. Ignored by governments who publicly state that the growing problem of street children in the Third World simply does not exist, and deprived of parental love, the police are often the only figures of authority that these youngsters come across. And even then it is an occasional dressing down for good form's sake.

Many of the street children have no families to return to; they are the displaced orphans of famine and war. They find fellowship and support among those in the same predicament. The gangs that spring up in the cities are predominantly male; girls are present but in smaller numbers. The reason for this is the esteem, or value, still attached to having a girl child around the house to cook and clean, or else the continuing practice in some cultures of paying a bride price to a girl's family when she is married off.

Kamau's Story

Male children, on the other hand, in a country such as Kenya (which has the highest birth rate in the world) are too often discarded, sent off to find their own way in the world, victims of the harsh economic stranglehold that condemns large sections of society in Third World countries to a life of poverty and need.

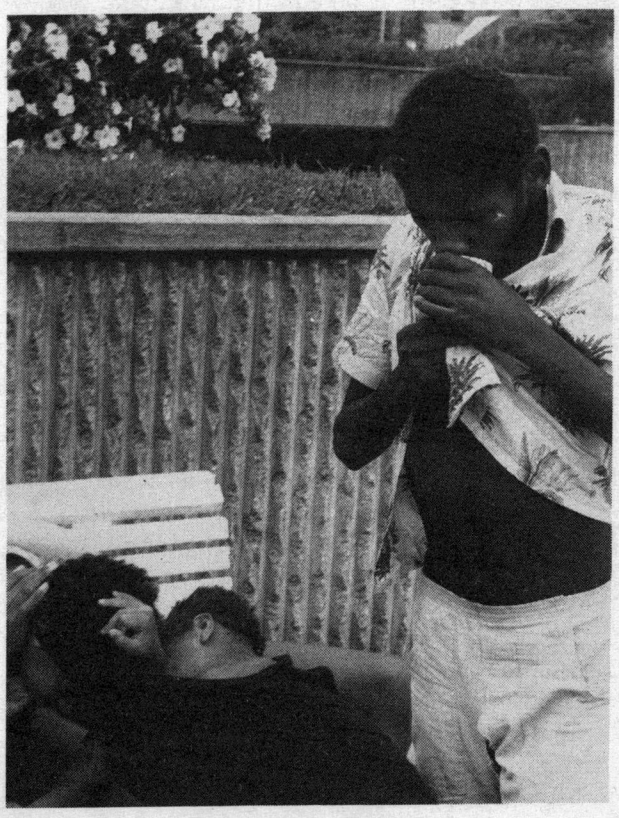

Kamau's story inspired three winning entries from writers who tried to think themselves into the life of a Nairobi street child. All three focused on his daily routine on the streets of the city. Ashley Parr (ten) summed up his pen portrait of Kamau by stressing what emerged as a central theme in the whole competition – the links in thoughts and interests that connect all children worldwide, whatever the differences in their backgrounds and circumstances.

Although their first-hand experience of the kind of hardships that Kamau and his friends endure daily was more or less non-existent, the compassion of children in this country was bottomless.

> *I'm Kamau, I clean cars in Nairobi,*
> *I clean them for exceedingly little money!*
> *I need this money to survive for food and rags.*
> *I bet the people in rich, fast cars,*
> *Never think of me when drinking in bars! . . .*
>
> *Do you ever wonder about me?*
> *Because I often wonder about you!*

Kyle Tebbitt (fourteen) pictured Kamau at risk amid the traffic.

> *The continuous growling of gleaming cars*
> *Streaming past.*
> *Once in you cannot stop,*
> *Like a maze, the walls crushing around you.*
> *Once caught you haven't a chance.*
> *Njoroge! No, please God no!*
> *Now just a bedraggled lump of flesh,*

Kamau's Story

*Lolled unceremoniously against the steel
   monsters . . .
Saying in his unheard words, "Now Kamau
   you're next".
Why do I exist in this life,
A living death in which I am encased?
Now,
I shall risk my life again . . .*

*I wish they'd just leave me be.
The continuous growling stream of gleaming
   cars,
Once caught, you haven't a chance.*

Polly Rance (also fourteen) concentrated on the unequal relationship between Kamau and those whose windows he cleaned.

*I am cleaning a car,
A huge silver monster that lies sleeping,
By the edge of the treacherous road.
The window opens, just a fraction.
I peep inside to where a man sits,
Eating fruit.
Hidden from the outside world,
In his refuge of shining chrome and soft leather.*

*He tires of the fruit, a mango,
And throws it into the road,
Where it is squashed to pulp
By another shining monster passing by.
Nobody cares.
That could have been my supper,
That could have been me.*

Hidden Hands

I am as common as the mango,
Just another common street child.
A disposable commodity.
If I were to die tonight,
They'd soon find someone else to clean their cars.

The image of Kamau going about his daily work with the ever-present threat of injury or death was an inspiring one for other entrants too. The threats posed by traffic are well known to all children the world over.

Kamau's Story

A bird drifts through the sky,
Like Kamau through the traffic.
He darts in and out but sees no danger,
Like a bird through clouds and kites.
His wet cloth glides over the silk paintwork,
Like a bird over the horizon.

Naomi Slinn, 14

I dodge round the vehicles,
Scamper about,
Both eyes wide open,
Alert, like a scout.

Kirsty Paterson, 11

With no homes, no security, and no one to care, the life of a street boy like Kamau is often a lonely one. The despair and the hardship of his days soon destroys any dreams of wealth, or illusions of a glamorous urban life.

I, Kamau, exist.
I have nothing to live for.
Nobody needs me.
I should be dead.

I sleep in the market-place,
Among the decaying fruit.
I shield myself with coarse sacking,
To comfort my overworked body,
From the cruel nights.

Wenna Jenkins, 14

*Car windows I clean all day and night,
There's no one there to tuck me up tight.
Can nobody see my terrible plight?*

Jimmy Pearce, 9

The street child's world is a primitive one. Unlike the authors of the poems, Kamau has no one to turn to when things go against him, no one to protect or feed him. To Kamau the world around him is a hostile place.

*I wander around,
Hoping someone will notice,
I'm down.
Down in the dumps.
That's where they want me,
I've no one to love me,
Even the police throw me around.*

Clare Hallahan, 8

*Alone, alone, with no one to turn to,
Surrounded by people, none of whom care
About me. And why should they?*

Rebecca Whittingham, 15

*The loneliness suddenly comes to my heart.
Sleeping in the doorways of shops,
And on the dirty park bench at night.
You cannot get to sleep at all.
All night long there is music, cars and noise.*

Zoe Birch, 10

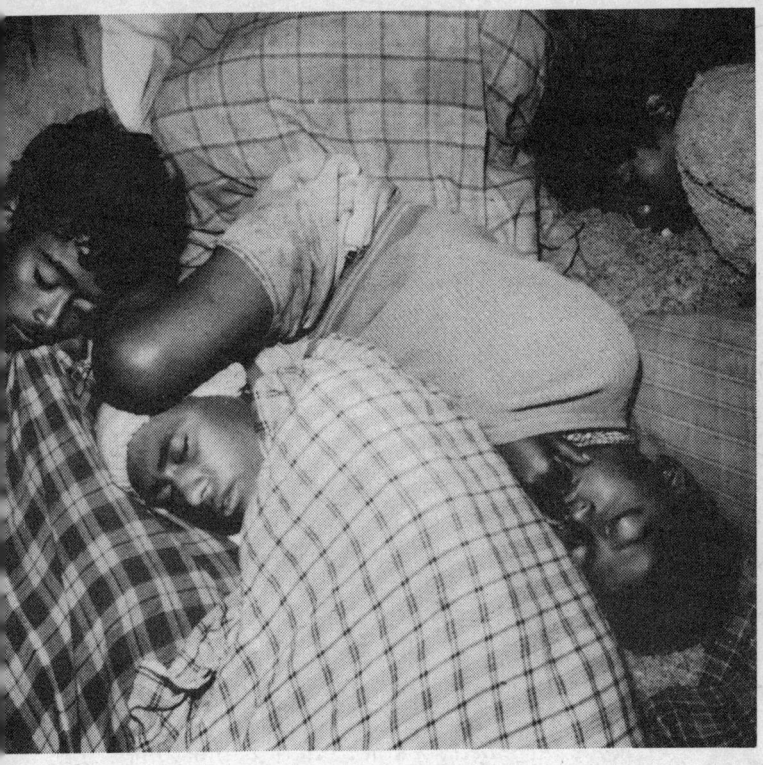

Kamau's predicament must make him feel angry and trapped, some thought...

Every day I long for my freedom,
Anger and hatred is all I feel for Europeans.
Why do they drive in posh cars,
Thinking they're good?
They give me a few coppers,
When they've got piles of money.
I'm a downcast child,
I'm inhuman.

John Paul Davies, 10

I am but an insignificant creature in a barred cage,
Its size ever decreasing – trapping me in.

Elizabeth Kruba, 14

... or else at the very bottom of the pile with everyone above oblivious to his suffering.

If I were a rich man, I'd help the poor.
If I belonged to the government I'd make the law,
But I am just a street boy.
The world is just a street,
It will never be more.

Alejandra Hormaeche, 11

As I sit here wondering about the world,
Imagining how everyone lives,
I think to myself "Where do I stand in this world?
Have I reached rock bottom or is there more to go?"

Daniel Jones, 16

But for his first months in Nairobi, Kamau was more fortunate than most. He found someone wiser, Njoroge, who took care of him and showed him both friendship and a way to make money. Although they don't have the academic opportunities or accomplishments of Western school children, these streetwise youngsters are cynics from an early age.

Kamau's Story

Whether they be in large gangs or in twosomes like Njoroge and Kamau, these teenagers are brought together in a common fight to survive in an unfriendly world. In some cities, the ghetto mentality of street children is so well developed that they have their own currency – elastic bands that are exchanged for food and drinks from friendly shopkeepers. When children don't have any money or elastic bands, their fellows will help them out. No one in the gang will starve.

The value of friendship in the face of distress was high on the list of poetic priorities. Njoroge played a vital role in Kamau's life.

I miss him.
I miss him when I have a good haul from a busy day,
Not being able to share the pressure with him.

Michelle Kelly, 13

However, the excitement of comradeship and the thrill of the city soon turned to anger and despair.

It was fun at first flying, flitting through the cars.
At night the headlights flashing on, they looked like shooting stars.
The great eight-wheeler roaring past like cyclones rushing by.
My friend and I laughed at them, we knew we'd never die.

Suzanne Wainwright, 12

Kamau's Story

Njoroge ran out when the lights turned red.
When suddenly they turned green, and he was
  dead.
The car he was washing when the lights turned
  green,
Didn't wait for him to finish his screen.

Susan Heath, 14

The brutal death of Njoroge, his only friend, had a powerful effect on the bemused and frightened Kamau.

He was lying there in front of me.
People looking and staring at me,
People gathered round looking down,
  wondering what to do.
Njoroge was dead.

Sarah Barch, 15

Death seized him far too young,
Left him lifeless, . . .

Chrystalla Mouskovias, 15

Without Njoroge Kamau was tempted to answer his loneliness and isolation by joining up with one of the large gangs of street children that he had seen roaming Nairobi. These groups – small societies that live, eat, sleep and even die on the streets of large cities in Third World countries – use the money they raise by petty crimes such as pickpocketing to buy food. But their independence, and the ease with which they make a living, often tempts them into more serious areas of crime. Theft, shoplifting, prostitution are common among these children, some as young as eleven. And with their ill-gotten gains they are urged by their peers to experiment with alcohol and drugs. A lethal cocktail of tablets and the vapours from petrol is a favourite in Nairobi. Would Kamau fall in with these ways?

> *I hunted around in search of food,*
> *But as usual there was none to be found.*
> *Quickly I made my way to the town,*
> *Without bothering to wash or change my clothes.*
>
> *I turned a corner and to my surprise*
> *I saw two bottles of milk on a doorstep.*
> *Without thinking if it was right or wrong,*
> *I grabbed them and fled.*
>
> Michael Buck, 12

Or did he resist because of his unease at doing wrong?

> *I may have to steal to get some food*
> *And eat it in alleyways.*
>
> *I don't want to steal,*
> *It would never do.*
> *I'd like to go back from this horrid life,*
> *And try to improve it too.*
>
> Richard Basiurski, 10

Kamau's Story

Dashing around the streets so fast,
I can't help thinking, wondering how long will it last.
What will I be doing in a few years' time?
I will probably be living a life of crime.

Nicholas Marchant, 10

A lifetime of poor food, no decent home, and little or no health care soon takes its toll on street children like Kamau. His life expectancy is dramatically lower than those who wrote about him, even if he does manage to avoid Njoroge's fate. Matthew Goodman (aged eight) contrasted his own expectation of good health with Kamau's thoughts.

If I get ill
I haven't got any money
To go into hospital.

And what of the future for Kamau? Streetwise and tough at fifteen, hardened by perhaps ten years of fighting on the streets to survive, he and the other street children of the Third World's major cities are deprived of any formal education. The only life skill they have developed is that of theft.

A start has been made in some cities like Nairobi and Khartoum, in neighbouring Sudan. There, voluntary centres set up by charities aim to give the children a roof over their heads at night, food, and, if they want it, the basics of a practical education that will allow them to find ways of feeding and providing for themselves other than crime.

But for all their life experience and hardship, these children remain youngsters, with a corresponding need for affection and love. His lost family is a source of bitterness and rejection for Kamau, some writers thought.

> *I have a family, but they don't really love me.*
> *Nobody seems to care anymore.*
>
> Charlotte Spacey, 14

> *I was the oldest,*
> *I was rejected.*
> *Unsatisfactory, imperfect.*
> *I felt dejected.*
>
> *I had to leave home.*
> *I felt such shame . . .*
>
> Catherine O'Shea, 13

> *Thrown out, rejected, my parents couldn't afford me.*
> *I have to be an adult before I want to be . . .*
>
> Karen Crowse, 14

However, for others the bonds that unite Kamau's family were stronger and more resilient in the face of hardship.

> *I knew I would never be as rich as some;*
> *I did not even care.*
> *All I wish for now all day,*
> *Is that I might see my lost family.*

Helen Demopoulos, 13

Torn between joining a street gang with its attendant dangers, or returning to an unpredictable welcome with his family, Kamau's future doesn't look too rosy.

*I would be better off dead,
At least in heaven there would be friends.*

Alissa Chappell, 8

*Why don't I just run into the road and
End this worthless life?
I often wish I had my own big flashy car.
That's the only thing I live for.
The only thing that stops me from doing it.*

Frances Brennan, 12

Kamau's Story

The car provided a link between the writers and Kamau – a common experience. In the case of the writers it was perhaps a family saloon. For Kamau it was the cars that he cleaned. These vehicles, especially those of wealthy foreign tourists, made a focus for Kamau's dreams of escape.

Why get run over when you can play?
That's what the better-off boys think and say,
But I lead a very different life,
For me it's all hard work . . .

Peter Hargraves, 11

I'm Kamau, and you're lucky, you know.
I have no fancy clothes to show.

George Riley, 10

We can play when we come from school,
And we can go to the swimming pool.
We can go to school and play,
They have to work all day.

Daniel Butcher, 9

The different attitudes to cars between the writers and Kamau stress the contrasts in their two life styles.

You have big cars and lots of money,
For you the days are always sunny.
Please let me clean your windows.

Matthew Pearce, 11

For Matthew Longcake (eight), Kamau's path to happiness was straightforward.

I wish I was richer,
Because then I'd have some friends.

Others found a more sophisticated, but none the less positive message in Kamau's plight.

His job is rather humble, cleaning people's cars
But a job's a job, and without it he would
probably starve.

Frances Henshaw, 12

I went to the hot dusty road and waited for a
car.
It was coming round the corner,
I jumped out to stop it,
It went past,
I felt sad and hungry.
Ten cars go by and not a nickel,
Then two drivers both paid me for cleaning
their screens.
I was rich.

Tom Davis, 8

And there was the expectation, be it distant and in either abstract or even material form, that a better future was coming for Kamau, when there would be justice and equal rights.

> *I know that one day,*
> *My situation will change.*
> *I'll be rich,*
> *And have a big car.*
>
> Sarah McTaggart, 14

> *I want to escape to a new life.*
> *Start afresh and grow . . .*
> *I could stow away in a tourist's car . . .*
>
> Paul Saunders, 15

> *I often dream of my life,*
> *If I took a hitch with one of those cars,*
> *Across the seas to the Western millionaires.*
> *Lands of happiness and contentment.*
>
> Anna Bunning, 15

> *I dream about being a wealthy child,*
> *And having a dad with a car*
> *For me to ride in instead of to clean.*
>
> James Baxter, 9

> *My life will change I hope one day.*
> *With the help of those who say they pray for justice*
> *In this unfair land.*
> *Hunger and poverty will then be banned.*
>
> Simon Learman, 13

I pray to my God every single day,
Please dear Lord, give me time to pray.
And let the world know our plight . . .

Simon Dougherty, 9

Otami's Story

The girl is just standing there. Leaning heavily on primitive crutches ... her left leg is terribly deformed, standing right out in the air, twisted, angling upwards. Such a monument of deprivation. Her grief is so tangible ... she just stands there silently in the midst of it.

    Liv Ullman, UNICEF Ambassador of Good Will, from *Choices* (Weidenfeld, 1985)

Otami clutched in terror the hand of the stranger who had brought her from the peace of a rural village to the ceaseless roar and bustle of Bangkok's main railway station.

The fisherwoman, as Otami's parents called her, had come to their village only yesterday and offered ten pounds in advance wages — a huge sum for the family. In return, thirteen-year-old Otami accompanied the woman with a kindly, maternal face to the bright lights of Thailand's main city, to work in a factory. It would only be for a year, they had promised her, and then she could come home.

Although Otami was broken-hearted to leave her home, her brothers and sisters, and the small school where she had begun to learn to read and write, the family desperately needed the money. A bad harvest had decimated their crop of rice, and her father had been forced to take to hunting in surrounding woods in order to find food for the table. The fisherwoman, with her cash and promises of more to follow, had been irresistible for the hard pressed family.

Otami is one of the estimated five hundred children who arrive in Bangkok to be sold every week. The peak of this influx of slave labour comes in the dry season – January, February and March. A large proportion of the children like Otami come from the Isan, the north-eastern sector of Thailand, where poor soil and a lack of water make agriculture a daily toil to scratch a meagre living.

Some children come to Bangkok under their own steam. Others are accompanied by a relative, who will take care of the business transaction before abandoning the youngster into the arms of a stranger.

Otami is the victim of a middleman – the fisherwoman, literally a fisher of children. In return for the ten pounds she gave Otami's parents, this merchant will now sell the child on the open market which booms around the station. Factory owners will pay between thirty-five and seventy-five pounds for a healthy youngster, boy or girl.

Once she sells Otami, that is very likely an end to the fisherwoman's toil. Her motherly and reassuring tones when leading Otami away from her home are soon forgotten in the commerical merry-go-round of the station market. The pledge to return her catch after one year is seldom honoured. Most middlemen don't give a second thought to the children once money has changed hands with a factory owner.

Those who do have scruples, according to their own code, are often given false addresses by purchasers, anxious to avoid the prying eyes of government child labour inspectors, who try without much success to enforce laws that could save Otami from her fate.

Otami, meanwhile, is led away from the station to a strange and frightening city to slave seven days a week, twelve hours a day, in a garment factory, for less than a pound a day. The suits she makes are then sold across the counters of elegant European stores for anything from thirty pounds to several hundred for the more elaborate items.

Otami sits cross-legged on the hard, cold floor of the stuffy, airless, cramped factory. Doors and windows are locked to keep honest eyes out, for fear that they may call in the inspectors.

Otami works silently alongside the nameless faces of other youngsters sewing hems and dreaming of home. All day long she pulls and pushes her needle through the fabric. Her fingers are cut to ribbons; even when the owner gives her a basic thimble to protect the scars and keep the blood off the garments, Otami is often too tired to care enough to put it on. Other older girls who are favourites of the factory owner are allowed to use the machines, but for Otami her daily toil is manual. Whatever she dreams to take her mind off the monotony and pain, the same unwelcoming floor of the factory will be her bed tonight after she has eaten a meagre meal of rice.

Despite a casebook of laws prohibiting child labour, one quarter of Thailand's workforce is aged between ten and fourteen, with cases recorded of workers as young as seven. By a sad paradox child labour is a self-perpetuating slavery for many poor Thais, for by selling their child to do an adult's work, the parents are in fact depriving themselves of a job, forcing themselves back into poverty, and ensuring that their children will continue to work to support the family.

Because of the casual appoach of middlemen and the treachery of factory owners, many children never see their parents again. They are simply lost in a mass of youngsters working in the city, impossible to detect even by the most determined of parents.

Otami's story prompted the biggest response from our poets, although none of the eight winners came from this section. The daily drudge of factory life, with its monotony, its atmosphere of fear and oppression, was a recurring and general theme.

The dingy back alleyways where rats scuttle,
Scavenging in the bins,
It can all be heard by Otami,
Who lays on the cold, concrete floor,
Shivering as if a gale were blowing around her.

The first glimmers of day
Infiltrate the greasy windows.
They must awaken,
Seeing as always the meagre meal set before them.
No one dares to complain
Or there will not be a last meal at the end of the day.

A young child near Otami cries out.
For she cannot straighten her back
In attention to the owner.
So she is quickly dragged away.
Her screams echo around the room,
And the fingers of fear touch everyone.

Lily Mo, 12

Morning now.
Got to get up.
Got to start work.
What's for breakfast?
Bread and water again.
I can't sit up,
My back hurts.
Get my towel and go for a wash.
Time to start.
Here comes the first pile of dresses.
Start now.
Must have done at least 30.
What time is it?
Only 9 o'clock . . . .
Now I've done 40 . . . 50 . . . 60 . . . 70 . . .
80 . . . 90 . . . 100

There goes the bell.
Time for supper.
Bread and water. Mmm.
I wish I could see my mum and dad.
And the rest of my family.
I hope that they are luckier than me.
Somebody is in my sleeping place.
Find somewhere else.
Here I think.
Yes!
It's warmer here anyway.
Ahh . . . sleep . . . sleep.

Lauren Grindrod and Catherine Melia, 9

Few outsiders have ever managed to get behind the locked doors and windows of Bangkok's sweatshops

Otami's Story

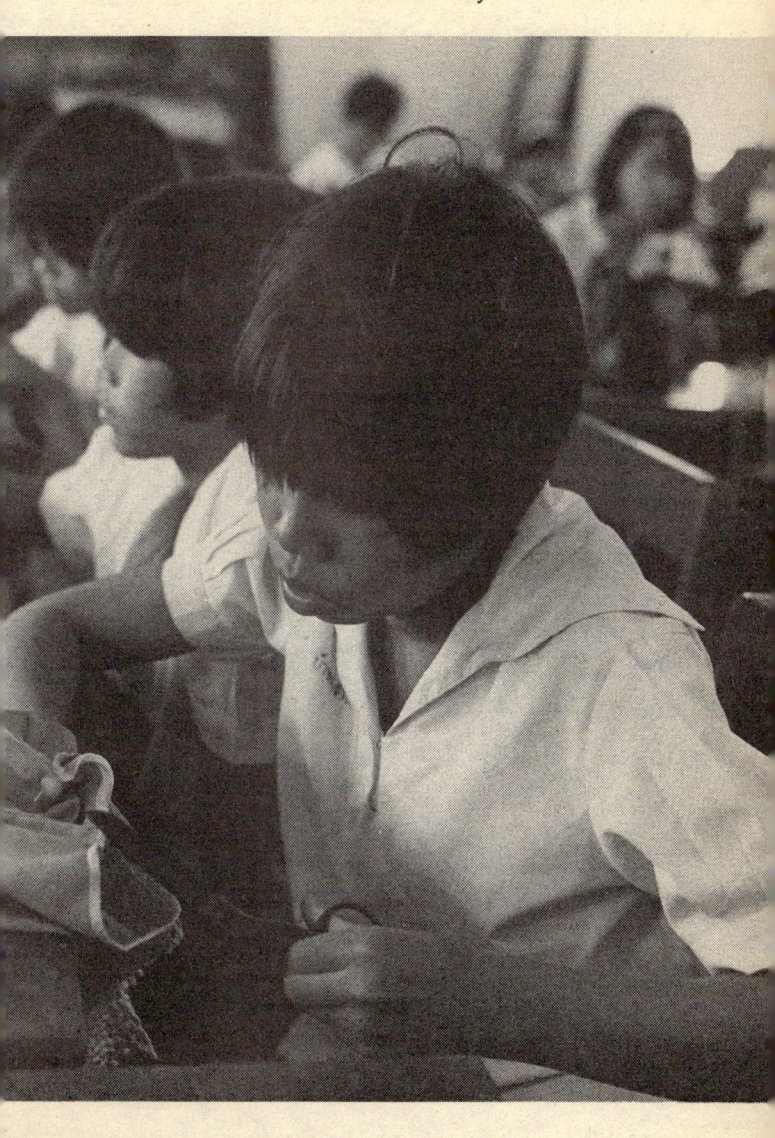

to see the misery of the young slaves who are imprisoned there. Occasionally the factory inspectors will swoop, and great play will be made in the press of "liberated children", but the exploitation of youngsters is a growing problem in Thailand, and there are few resources to combat this effectively.

> *It's like a prison camp working twelve hours at a time,*
> *No break or rest, like I've committed a crime.*
>
> Charlotte Stone, 14

> *Sewing hems on rich people's suits,*
> *It's worse than being an army recruit.*
>
> Sarah Cain, 10

Otami's Story

When police and inspectors have gained entry into Bangkok's sweatshops they have found scenes of extreme cruelty where laws, prohibiting the use of child labourers, are flaunted in the remorseless pursuit of maximum profits.

*The day is hot, the night is clear,
Thailand and Asia's children work, in sweatshops near.
They sleep on floors as cold as ice,
And all they eat is a bowl of rice.*

Anne-Marie Byrne, 11

*Our eyes down, our bodies bent,
Our life's blood draining just to make a cent.
We rarely speak, we haven't time,
We work in the sweatshops just to make a dime.*

David Pennick, 13

*In the city,
The children work,
For their survival.*

*So they work in,
The need to live,
Another day.*

Georgina Mwale, 16

The children's tasks are ceaseless. Often they are beaten by their employers if they are slow at the work, or make mistakes and waste material. The sweatshop is engulfed in a time warp where the seven-day working week offers no landmarks other than sleeping, eating and working.

> *The air a stifling blanket of fibres,*
> *Endless yards of fabric blur.*
>
> *I wonder what day it is,*
> *As if it matters. They are all alike.*
>
> Lucy Braga, 13

> *Sewing machines buzzing all day long,*
> *Making life a weary song.*
>
> Sinead Heekin, 11

> *Face hot, sweat cold,*
> *Hands darting, pushing needle in, pulling needle out.*
> *Back aches, legs ache, why?*
> *On and on ceaselessly, never stopping.*
> *Can't breathe, too hot.*
> *Breath catches, choke.*
>
> Louise Charter, 14

Health is a luxury few child labourers enjoy for long. Even if they arrive healthy after a lifetime in the countryside, like Otami, the sweatshop environment soon affects them. Otami has seen others – victims of unhygienic conditions and cruel overwork – carried out of the factory screaming. She is worried about her own fate. Poor food – plain rice as infrequently as once a day is the staple diet, with a weak fish-head sauce as a special treat – combines with general airlessness and lack of bathing facilities in the tropical heat of Bangkok to accelerate the onset of chest complaints, chronic nausea, swollen legs and the like, while aged machines take their toll on the unskilled fingers and limbs of those entrusted with their operation.

*I can never remember having enough to eat,
It's like a trip to heaven when I taste cooked meat.
Bread and water is my daily diet,
Some people steal, but I dare not try it.*

Ophelia Matthias, 13

*My hair is starting to fall out,
And soon I'll be bald.
My life is starting to crumble . . .*

Scott Cheesman, 14

*My back is like a rotting piece of wood,
I've got cramp.
I feel like a machine.*

Tom Sadowski, 10

*Cold stone slabs, no cover, no hope.
I work until I can work no longer.
But I must.
Each day my back gets worse,
A cough developing – colder and colder.*

Dawn Hodkins, 16

46   *Hidden Hands*

Otami's Story

The stone floor of the factory is Otami's sleeping place. No mattress or mosquito nets ease aching limbs or prevent infection in the sweltering heat. Used to comfortable beds and often the luxuries of their own bedroom, the spartan nature of Otami's sleeping arrangements made a particular impression on writers, giving them an object on which to base their contrasts between their own life style and that of Otami.

I sleep on a cold stone floor,
No blankets, no warmth, no comfort at all.
No one there to tuck me in,
No one there to tickle my chin.
There's no one, no one to love me at all.

Olivia Fallowes, 14

The tiled, slippery floor in the dull dusty room,
Is filled with black slimy grease.

Sharon Tubbritt, 11

For some writers the causes of Otami's distress were plain and clear. A finger was pointed at the factory owner.

The people who I work for are very cruel to me,
They treat me like their personal slave.
They think I'm just a big machine,
Who does their work for them.

Timothy Jones, 10

> Our boss is scared of paying us,
> In case we run away in a rush.
>
> Andrew Wood, 9

> I'm trying hard to convince myself I'm having a dream.
> But no! I know it's real.
> I'm being poked by a grotesque man wearing gold rings and bracelets.
>
> Catherine Lowe, 15

Others, however, considered Otami a victim of forces rather closer to home.

> At 14 years cross-legged I sit.
> Making suits and hoping they'll fit.
> Those big ladies in the UK,
> If they only knew they'd been made this way.
>
> Marie Carter, 15

> I wonder if the woman who wears it will consider me.
> If we should ever meet,
> I wonder if she would want to speak to me . . .
>
> Madelaine Elliott, 12

> Children working, there's no rest.
> Making shirts, socks and vests.
> Work is all we ever do,
> Making all these clothes for you!
>
> Joanne Burke 9

Otami's Story

There is a huge difference between the sweatshops producing the dresses and suits, and the high street shops in the West that sell them on to an unsuspecting public.

"Mummy, that looks a lovely dress,"
The acrylic suit so neat and trim.
"For £25 it says."
"Made in Thailand the label says."
"Buy it mum."
Oh, posh, extravagant lady, would you buy,
A dress made by the childish labour, the bitter tears,
And hopeless future of
Poor young Otami.

Emma Cookson, 13

While my hands worked mechanically with needle and thread,
I sent my eyes to England and watched a man sell a suit.
To a wealthy lady who hoped it would match,
The new creamy jacket she'd found in a sale.

"Such a charming colour, how stylish, and elegant,
So perfect for madam, I must recommend it,
It's made by girls in India, you know."

The lady clasped her hands and squealed,
"Oh, how sweet, how lovely.
I've always wanted to sew,
Never got round to it myself, you understand."

*She tottered out of the shop feeling pleased with
  her purchase.
Clinked into her limousine and drove away.
Well fancy lady, give me your elegant fashion,
Your expensive car and your wealthy life style,
And come to India where you can sew forever,
Twelve hours a day, seven days a week.
Sew and sew until your fingers are throbbing,
Sore from blunt needles, worn down to the
  bone.
Sew until your back breaks on the cold stone
  floor,
One pound a day, if you're lucky.*

*But you wouldn't mind, you've always wanted
  to sew.
You never got round to it,
Did you?*

Johanna Quincey, 14

Otami's Story

Thoughtless people who wear these clothes,
They don't think of me sitting here.
All they think of is how pretty they look in them.

Katherine Handman, 11

A bad harvest, a minor thing,
For those of you who like kings,
Set me on the road for Bangkok.
Ever since then I have been in this pen,
Slogging and working for life.

Gavin Doyle, 14

A number of writers pointed out that it was no good bemoaning Otami's plight, and then exploiting her labour by buying the product of her toil in high street shops. There is a direct link between our consumer desires and the conditions of Bangkok's sweatshops.

> *Thousands gather round to take pity on me,*
> *Sad but not disturbed, hearing without listening.*
> *They are closed in and sheltered by their world of affluence.*
>
> *I have nothing to lose, nothing to gain.*
> *Who am I to stand up?*
> *Who am I to have an opinion?*
> *I'm just a downtrodden worker with no obligation.*
>
> Geneineve Archdeacon, 14

Another aspect of the links between those in the developed Western countries and exploited youngsters in Third World cities lies in the fact that Bangkok is a hugely popular tourist destination for visitors from Europe and America. While thousands gaze at the wondrous temples and are carried around the floating markets in traditional craft, Otami slaves away in areas of the town that are either off the visitors' itineraries, or are hidden from view in the heart of this vast capital.

> *They flock like birds to view our sights . . .*
> *They close their eyes, they don't want to see,*
> *The backstreet life . . .*

Otami's Story

These flocks that view a country rare,
Are they blind, or don't they care?
I make the clothes that clad their backs,
The frocks that line their high street shops.
Oh God, if they could only see, the gnawing
  pain inside of me!

Sophie Weed, 15

The theme of "them and us" was central to the entire competition. While a thirteen-year-old in this country spends five days a week in the classroom, Otami, despite laws demanding that Thailand's children get a similar education for at least seven years, has to work. Legislation is simply ignored, and the realities of her life bear little resemblance to the wishes of those who run the government. Several writers imagined themselves, with their knowledge of a privileged life, into the place of Otami and the girls on the factory's stone floor.

I would not be able to change my clothes at all.
I would not know my sums.
I would not be able to do joined up writing.
I would not have any maths to do.
I would just have sewing to do.

Rebecca Garretty, 8

Look at the poor children on the floor
I'm joining them today
Look at them sewing away.

Jenny Cammilin, 9

*Here I am,
Sitting on my chair.
There she is,
Sitting on a hard floor . . .
Here I am doing my maths,
There she is doing her sewing . . .
Here we can talk to all our friends,
She can't talk to anyone.
Here I am with my family,
There she is with nobody.*

Dominique Jones, 9

Whatever the privations of her daily life, Otami cannot be deprived of her dreams and her hopes. Focusing on the goods she produces each day, Otami tries to imagine where they are heading.

*I've often thought about running away.
I could hide in a box with all the clothes and
   suits,
And be taken to London with ladies' dresses
   and boots.*

Marianne Garvey, 10

*I have slowly closed myself in.
I seek refuge in myself, for I can find no comfort
   in the real world.
I helplessly dream of wearing these clothes I
   make,
Living the lives of the rich people who shall buy
   them,
In their fine houses, riding in fancy cars.*

Helen Cresswell, 14

Otami's Story

Otami's family, her home in the distant Isan, are never forgotten. Despite the situation into which she has been abandoned by that same family, her love for them remains.

I want to leave this horrible place,
But I cannot, for my parents' sake.

Vanessa Edwards, 9

My three brothers, my two sisters,
Do they miss me?
Do they know the things I go through,
With no rice for tea?

Rebecca Smith, 9

I clutched the little silver pendant,
The only thing I owned apart from memories.
I still remember that day when all my mother's problems disappeared.

We have no money, no rice, she pleaded,
The children will have to work.
It rang out in my head over and over again.

Michelle Watkinson, 13

But some day, somehow, some time,
I'll see my parents again.
And when I see them again,
The crops will be strong, good and filling.
And I won't have to work,
In this dull, small, hot, noisy, ear-deafening factory.

Tresa Begley, 11

56   *Hidden Hands*

For some writers, Otami's dreams owed more to their own story books than to anything she might have experienced. They transported her to a land of fantasy, and then back to earth with a bump.

> *Sitting in the sweatshop on a hot summer's day,*
> *Dreaming of a handsome prince who will take her away.*
> *But of course no prince came,*
> *And she came back to life, and it was just the same.*

Geraldine Baxter, 11

Otami's Story

Down in the cellar, deep, dark, down,
I hear Otami singing, what a lovely soft sound.
By the fire I sit and dream,
And in the flames I see pictures,
Of wonderful things that
Never come to me!
People fat, people thin, but all
Dressed well with clothing covering their skin.
A flowing silver cloak?
But just then the shopkeeper
Calls, the embers move, my dreams
Go up in smoke!

Nicola McLeary, 10

When trying to forget her situation in dreams, Otami regards her life in the sweatshop with a mixture of resignation, exhaustion and anger. Her daily toil stretches out without end.

I've a sore throat, and a tight chest.
You owe me money!
Anger's growing deep inside.
Tears are hard to hold back.

Catherine Brewerton, 8

Am I stuck here for ever?
Bent back and poor pay.
I'm tired.
I watch the stitches go in and out.
Silently rocking me to sleep.

Siobhan Tighe, 10

Most of them come here as young children.
They leave in a coffin.
Old and decrepit
Hunchbacks of life.

Antonia Mulvey, 13

Oh where is the light?
At the end of the tunnel someone said,
At the very end of my tunnel is no light, only night.
And very soon I will be dead
Laid on my deathbed of rags and old dustbags.

Hannah Smith, 14

The money I get, I send away
The pain I keep.
The love I need is gone for ever.
But the pain is here to stay.

Maria Cocker, 13

Andrelina's Story

Why can't they see that supermarkets stuffed with thirty-five different brands of chocolate bars, and twenty-two assorted breakfast cereals are the reason why most people in most countries don't know what a chocolate bar is, and don't eat breakfast at all?

> Father John Medcalf
> (Padre Juan Luis)
> Letter from Nicaragua
> *Catholic Herald* 14th August 1987

Dawn finds nine-year-old Andrelina slipping silently out of the warm bed that she shares with her two older brothers. Still half asleep, she goes to collect some water, and prepares breakfast for her brothers and parents. It is a simple meal – similar to that which will be eaten by many other poor Brazilian families this morning and every morning – of manioc bread, prepared the night before with gravelly, rough flour, and perhaps a few beans.

She rouses the rest of the family reluctantly from their sleep. They wash and then eat in silence. Clutching hold of her treasured hat, Andrelina follows on as the four older, larger figures leave their home in the grey light of early morning, to wait on the nearby main road for the battered truck that will bounce and rattle them to the sugar plantation where they work from dawn to dusk.

Andrelina, dressed in rags, with a wide-brimmed sun hat several sizes too big for her, stands in the fields of cane wielding a machete, a broad, heavy, knife. Despite her frail arms and thin, malnourished body, she works alongside her family – they operate as a team felling the crop and gathering it in bundles.

Andrelina's Story

The harvest goes on for about six months every year. When there isn't any sugar cane to cut, they work clearing the land and weeding, picking out the stones. They are paid according to the amount of cane they collect during the day; every minute counts, and even at the height of the day, when the sun is burning down, Andrelina's father is reluctant for his family to stop for a rest. When he does consent, his daughter goes off in search of a little shade and sits sucking a piece of cane to renew her strength for the afternoon ahead.

Occasionally she will pause to look around the plantation, and smile at other children at work, or rest, nearby. Some are just babies, strapped in a coarse harness to their mother's back as she works. Others, of the same age as Andrelina, smile back, but all are too tired to play, or even to talk. They have to conserve their energies. In the sugar cane producing state of Paraiba some 40 per cent of the workers on plantations are under eighteen years of age, with 10 per cent under twelve.

Andrelina's daily toil is not only arduous, but fraught with dangers. A badly aimed machete, especially in the hands of a tired and unskilled child of just nine years of age, can maim for life. There is no first aid kit available on the plantation to deal with even the most minor of cuts. Andrelina has grown used to the sight of blood and open wounds.

Sores, particularly on the hands, blisters and stiff backs cannot be given a rest. The scrapes and grazes soon become infected, allowing more serious problems to set in; sometimes limbs are lost in this way.

The sugar cane crop is sprayed with chemicals to protect it from insect infestation. Some of the chemicals used have been banned in western European countries because of the health hazards they carry with them. Runny eyes, and, more seriously, rashes and sores, can be all too common lasting side effects.

A bleak but welcome hooter marks the end of the day's labours as dusk falls. Tired, hot and sticky, Andrelina drags herself slowly to the ancient truck while her father collects the family's earnings from the foreman. This averages out at about £2.50 a day.

Collapsing exhausted into the back of the vehicle as it bumps and jolts along the way home, Andrelina sleeps soundly, resting on her favourite brother's shoulder.

Their corrugated iron home is a tied cottage, owned by the plantation bosses and standing in a row; the foreman lives at the end. A small piece of land is attached. Its poor soil yields a few vegetables, perhaps some beans, but for the main part is given over to chickens and a goat. Andrelina feeds the animals while her mother begins to prepare the supper. The little girl then trudges off to fetch water for the family to wash away the dirt of the day. And then they sit down to eat – more manioc bread, but this time freshly made, beans, perhaps some chicken to supplement the diet.

As a rule Andrelina is just too tired to stay awake after she has eaten. In the evenings, there is a school for the young children who have to work, run by a local church. But Andrelina often simply doesn't have enough energy to go. After a day's work on the plantation, her undernourished body aches to rest.

Andrelina's Story

Before falling asleep she will often talk and daydream with her brother, João, who is just three years older. Together they fantasize about escape from their drudgery – to the nearby city, to the bright lights. If they could learn to read and write, they could get good jobs. But when they wake up the next day nothing has changed.

Based in the north-east of Brazil around the states of Pernambuco and Paraiba, the sugar industry makes extensive use of child labour to harvest the cane.

Families like Andrelina's live in virtual slavery, although this practice was officially abolished in Brazil almost a hundred years ago. But, like other laws which dictate that Andrelina should have a basic education and health care, they are ignored, because the state does not provide an inspectorate to police the cane fields.

The establishment – political and economic – has little interest in enforcing regulations. The sugar industry is a vital, and largely domestically owned, arm of the country's industry. Almost half the crop is used in refineries to produce a variation of alcohol which is used widely in the nation's cars in place of expensive foreign-produced petrol. The sweet smell of the refineries is well known to the *clandestinos*, the day labourers whose toil remains literally clandestine, secret, ignored by the authorities, in the fields which often border the industrial plants.

Andrelina's story, which mirrors that of the estimated two million children who work on the sugar plantations of north-east Brazil, inspired four of the winners of the *Catholic Herald* – CAFOD competition.

Ruth Lythe, at six, one of the youngest entrants, concentrated on the daily toil of the plantation.

> *My name is*
> *Andrelina and*
> *I have to chop*
> *Sugar cane*
> *Swing chop*
> *Swing chop*

Andrelina's Story

I am hot and
thirsty
Swing chop
Swing chop

Dusk is here
Swing chop
Swing chop
Now I go home
Swing chop
Swing chop

Lucy Carroll, aged ten, and Sarah Hicks, aged twelve, described Andrelina's thoughts and hopes throughout the working day.

I am Andrelina,
I work all day and night,
Why should I do this?
Why don't I get much pay?

I live with my poor family,
I cut the sugar here,
For all the wealthy people,
Madam, miss, sir.

My grandmother worked here,
And her mother too.
Maybe my children will work here.
Get paid little for what they do.

How can I escape this?
How can I get paid more?
We all get so little,
That's what makes us poor.

Why should I live here?
Why can't I get away?
Away from all this work, work, work,
It's all work, never play.

I'm just the same as anyone,
Rich, royal, poor,
I need to escape all this,
But my family and I are poor.

* * * * * *

As I awaken, my spirits are low.
The day ahead is hard and slow.

And not even the sun with her smiling face
Can wipe away the faintest trace
Of sadness that is in my heart!
The fear that I will never part,
From this laborious life of cutting cane,
Through all weathers, sun and rain.
But now I mustn't linger long.
I must get up, get up and on.
To make the meagre breakfast we have
And be out on the bus by five a.m.

As the bus bumps along, my mind begins to wander.
I dream of a life, a far cry from my own,
Where I have money I can squander.
Where my life is full of pleasure
And I have possessions I can treasure.
Where I can do just as I please
With no one to force me to my knees.
And tell me to cut harder, to cut more cane,
Ignoring all that searing pain.
A life that I can call my own
With food and love and a good home.

But as the day drags on and on,
I realize that my dream has gone.
My life of misery will always be.
And that I must face the reality.
I must make the best of what I have,
My parents and brothers and their love.
But as the end of the day draws near,
That faintest trace of hope is here.
That maybe, one day, I'll be free.
My family and I at liberty . . .

Francesca Collins, at fifteen the oldest of the winners, took as her focus the heavy machete and the cane of the sugar fields.

I swiped my machete with boredom
At the innocent cane.
The cane was like me
It grew into its form
And was then cruelly taken
And used by others without question.
Like me, it had no hope for other life.
Like me, it was not allowed to think.
But I did . . .
Would life ever change?
Would the hundreds of sugar cane humans
Always be ripped from their rightful roots?
And every bit of energy sucked from their ripe
   bodies?
Until nothing was left except their growing
   children,
So the torture could be repeated.

The seven-day-a-week, dawn-to-dusk routine of Andrelina's life, and its hardships, were a common theme.

I must not rest, I must not play,
Or the pennies I earn will be taken away.
At home we have some simple food,
Some beans and rice to do us good.
But first I must go to a nearby well,
And fetch water for the place where I dwell.
I clean the pots, I lay the fire,
But to have a rest is my desire.

Sarah Chambers, 10

Andrelina's Story

In the morning I get up at six o'clock,
On the bus, vroom, vroom, bump, bump.

Saskia Corder, 6

My family and I, we work as a team,
Like a metronome our chopping rings.

Susie Berrill, 14

Each reed of cane I cut,
Marks another hope destroyed.

Suzanna French, 13

*I get up in the morning at five,
And I say to myself I'm lucky to be alive.
Even though I'm hungry and feeling tired.
At least I've been hired.*

Kirsten Fernandez, 10

*I don't wake up and wonder
What the day has in store.
I know, the same. For ever.*

Daniela Bertoldin, 11

The combined earnings of Andrelina's family just about manage to feed the family each week. Without her labour, they would go without food. As it is, malnutrition is rife in north-east Brazil, and given the arduous work that young bodies are called upon to perform this can rapidly develop into more serious and life-threatening diseases.

Rates of pay for day labourers in the sugar fields are negotiated each year with the plantation owners by workers' representatives, but these figures are soon eaten into by Brazil's soaring inflation. Most families spend around 80 per cent of their income on food, with even a bag of sugar, made from the very cane they cut, costing them the equivalent of three or four hours' work.

*The South American power people
Let the mouths of us go sour
To set the money rolling in.
Money that we are cheated of.*

Denis de Reland, 15

Andrelina's Story

Laws on minimum safety requirements are ignored, leaving the workers to face a variety of lethal dangers every day.

*I am now aware of the slashing of the machetes
   getting closer.
A flash of steel strikes down before my eyes.
As I jump back with fear, my senses I now
   regain.*

Richard Collins, 12

*The arc of the blade.
The air thrashing by.
The short, sharp, swipe.
The echoing cry . . .*

*Catching my mouth,
Holding it back,
Minutes are lost.
For the courage I lack.*

*Somebody wake me,
Somebody wake me.
Arise me from my slumber.
No more can I bear.*

*The clanging of the metal,
The sharpening of steel,
The shape of the kettle,
Silhouette of a meal.*

*The life of a reaper,
A reaper of doom,
Is death and destruction,
Sorrow and gloom.*

Michael Atkinson, 14

Hidden Hands

The chemicals hurt my eyes.
I expect I had a spark of happiness.
The world glistens under God's sky.
I was boiling, exhausted, poor.

Claire Findlay, 6

The unions who negotiate wages for the workers have little power to protect them in reality, while the legal aid centres set up by the churches and voluntary bodies are few and far between. On top of that, they still have to cope with the suspicion and fear of poor families, used for generations to being exploited by their employers without a murmur of protest.

Andrelina and her family
Battle on the plantation

Andrelina's Story

From seven to seven
From dawn to dusk.
When the moon awakes thousands of sugar
  cane soldiers
Bleed on the ground.

She tells her brother
"If we could sell all of this think of
All the things we could buy"
The moon is watching
The sugar cane die.
The vultures appear from nowhere
Clapping their hands:
The owner takes a bunch
The speculator takes some more
The shipowner, the sugar company,
The supermarket and the corner shop.
Andrelina is going home.
Father counts the escudos
She the blisters and thorns.

Cleso Vorel, 12

Although half of the cane produced on Brazil's sugar fields goes to make alcohol-fuel, the rest is refined into the white crystals that find their way on to European and American breakfast tables. This link between them and us, between the writers and Andrelina and her family, was seized upon by many.

The people who eat the sugar I cut,
Are probably overweight.
And I am working all day long,
To make them be that way.

Anon, 13

*While they grow fat eating sugar,
I grow thin from pain.*

Kate Elson, 11

*So please, please help me,
And do not buy the sugar
You put in your tea.*

*Because you buy it cheap,
When the price should be very high.
Because of the work we put in,
That makes us nearly die!*

Rachel McCawley, 11

The burdens and injustices of Andrelina's life could only make her despair for the future, some writers thought.

Andrelina's Story

Despair engulfs me with its hand of inescapable agony,
As we draw near to the place where our burden lies.
Looking into the sky, I am relieved from the torment and sorrow of our lives
As I imagine how sweet freedom would be.
But once again, the calmness of the sky has tricked me,
For I realize where I am,
And the sound of frantic, hacking machetes echoes through the still air.
And I begin to wonder how the sugar cane could ever taste sweet.

Dina De Simone, 12

Each morning the sun rises
In the skies, not my heart,
For I know my world and I
Will never be set apart.

I know that no phantom sister
Or distant brother, I know,
Will ever take over a life of hell,
So that I can pack and go.

Andrea Enston, 13

The more I cut the more I earn,
The more I live the more I learn.
That I'll be here for the rest of my life,
Using the machete like a great big knife.

Paula Dunne, 12

The fields of cane so sweet to some,
So bitter to us.
Where does it stretch to?
Does it never end?
A sea of green wells over my head.
We're drowning in an ocean of poverty.

Michele Kidd, 14

Others imagine instead that Andrelina and her brother would hatch dreams and plans of escape in those twilight hours before they fell asleep.

I talk with my brother
About how I could escape.
He said he had tried,
But there was just more fields.

Angela Ferrari, 10

But we've got to think positive,
There's not much else to do.
Because there's worse off than us,
Yes, it's true.
But that's what we live on,
Just hopes and dreams.
For there is no end to this work,
Or so it seems.

Michelle Aitken, 12

Another day has been and gone,
But still I keep hoping . . .

Dale Fleming, 11

In fact most of those who do survive the perils of dangerous working conditions and malnutrition, and make it into their twenties, spend the rest of their lives on the plantation. Life expectancy is around 40 to 50 under the daily burden of such heavy manual work. For the young who do escape to the big cities like Recife, they exchange one type of exploitation for another. In the towns, with minimal education and little idea of how to survive in an urban context, they end up either as poorly paid domestic servants, nurturing dreams of their childhood in the country, or else as petty criminals and prostitutes.

However, for children in Britain, Andrelina's hopes and fantasies were about growing rich, and putting the world to rights.

> *But one day I shall leave*
> *All the work at home and field.*
> *Then travel very far*
> *And become wealthy as others.*
> *But I shall keep one thing in mind*
> *And that is to think of the poor.*
>
> Lainab Aschkar, 14

> *I hope that one day man's malicious ways*
> *Will change, and the world will see happier days.*
> *Until those times, which I hope I will see,*
> *I will try to endure this harsh, monotonous eternity.*
>
> Bernadette Abdalla, 15

> *Once I am away from the sugar cane fields,*
> *I still have a hard life making breakfast and doing other chores*
> *I am not sick of life though.*
> *I still have my family and others are not so fortunate.*

Andrelina's Story

My day comes to an end in the best possible
  way for me.
When I am sleeping I dream and pray to Jesus
Of a better life, for better conditions, for better
  food.
And for more fairness and equality in the
  world.

Jonathan Norburn, 10

On a more practical and immediate level, development agencies such as CAFOD and Oxfam, working in harmony with the local Catholic Church in north-east Brazil, are striving to bring education to working children, and to attack illiteracy rates of around 43 per cent. Health care facilities have also been made a priority, as well as legal centres where workers can be advised on the rights and wrongs of their employers' actions.

The family unit remains a strong force, and a source of great mutual support.

. . . my mother smoothes my hair.
I pretend not to have a care.
Then off to the fields with our parcels we go,
Me, Andrelina, and my brothers in tow.
The work is hard, our wounds are sore,
But our foreman wants us to cut much more.
Mother will bathe our hands when we return,
Love is what she gives, it's what we earn.
Love and smiles will take the pain away,
And tomorrow . . . well tomorrow is another
  day.

Helen Thompson, 10

And as well as the family, there is faith. Brazil has one of the largest Roman Catholic populations in the world.

It's very hard working here.
We have no money,
I wish God could help us.
He does a little bit. But He will help us,
Because He is a good friend,
He loves us very much, Our Father.

Kelly Abbott, 9

*And when her work is done,
She turns to the sun and says,
Thank you God for the day.*

Alison Cunningham, 6

Thank you God for the sugar cane.

Kate, 6

Child Labour
by *Joanna Moorhead*

If I ever owned a factory I'd make sure all the workers had enough to eat and somewhere to sleep at night. I'd never beat them and I'd give them weekends off and a holiday every year.

Sayan (13), former sweatshop worker in Bangkok

For Sayan himself, things could hardly have been more different. He spent three years of misery in a tiny, cramped textile factory. Constantly hungry, always exhausted and often beaten and abused, he worked on average fifteen hours a day. His pay was peanuts, about a quarter of the sum an adult would have expected for similar work. Days off were rare, and he was never allowed to leave the factory.

Happily, Sayan's nightmare is now behind him. He was one of eighteen children rescued from the factory by police after someone complained about conditions there. Today, he has a place in a church-run school, and for the first time his prospects look bright.

Not all other child workers are so lucky. For millions of youngsters around the world, the cycle of toil, danger, violence and exploitation continues unchecked.

These children are no isolated few. There are millions of them in many countries. But though so many in number they are largely invisible – locked away in back-street sweatshops or cut off on the vast plantations that are worlds unto themselves.

To us in Britain, the idea of treating children in such an appalling way is quite repugnant. Yet it is us – you and me! – who make child labour profitable. We are the ones who buy the goods – the instant coffee, the teabags, the granulated sugar, the tinned pineapple, even the cheap cotton and silk dresses – produced by child labour. We provide the market that sustains their work.

Even more ironic is the fact that these children who service our needs have so little themselves. The youngsters who pick our food are almost certainly undernourished. The teenage girls who sew our skirts, shirts and jackets wear rags themselves. And the young boys who hawk newspapers to tourists in exotic holiday spots are rarely able to read the words they sell.

This chapter examines the phenomenon of child labour in the world today, and looks at what can be done to end the enormous suffering it causes.

What is Child Labour?

"Child labour" sounds a straightforward enough concept. It means a child who works, doesn't it? But

Child Labour

what do we classify as childhood? When does adult life start – is it at 14, 16, 18 or even 21? And who decides? – should it be up to international law, or is it best for countries to continue to legislate for themselves?

Second, what precisely counts as labour? Does a twelve-year-old British girl washing her parents' car count as child labour? In this country it is usually considered laudable for children to be introduced to the discipline of work through occasional tasks done for their parents or others. And again, would we call a young boy in a Kenyan village collecting firewood for his mother a child labourer? Far more sensible, surely, to consider him as a youngster making a suitable and valuable contribution to the family home.

So work cannot be said to be universally a bad thing for children. In some societies, particularly in rural areas, children work to prepare themselves for productive adult lives. They work to increase their knowledge of the skills they will one day need in order to survive, and to gain status as useful members of the community. Work, for them, has an educative, rather than exploitative, dimension.

But in the sense in which the term is usually used, and in the sense we are concerned with here, child labour is a scourge, and has no advantages for the youngsters involved. It is about children as young as three or four years old being made to work many hours each day for little or no pay. It is about youngsters under the age of ten or in their early teens having to spend their days in environments

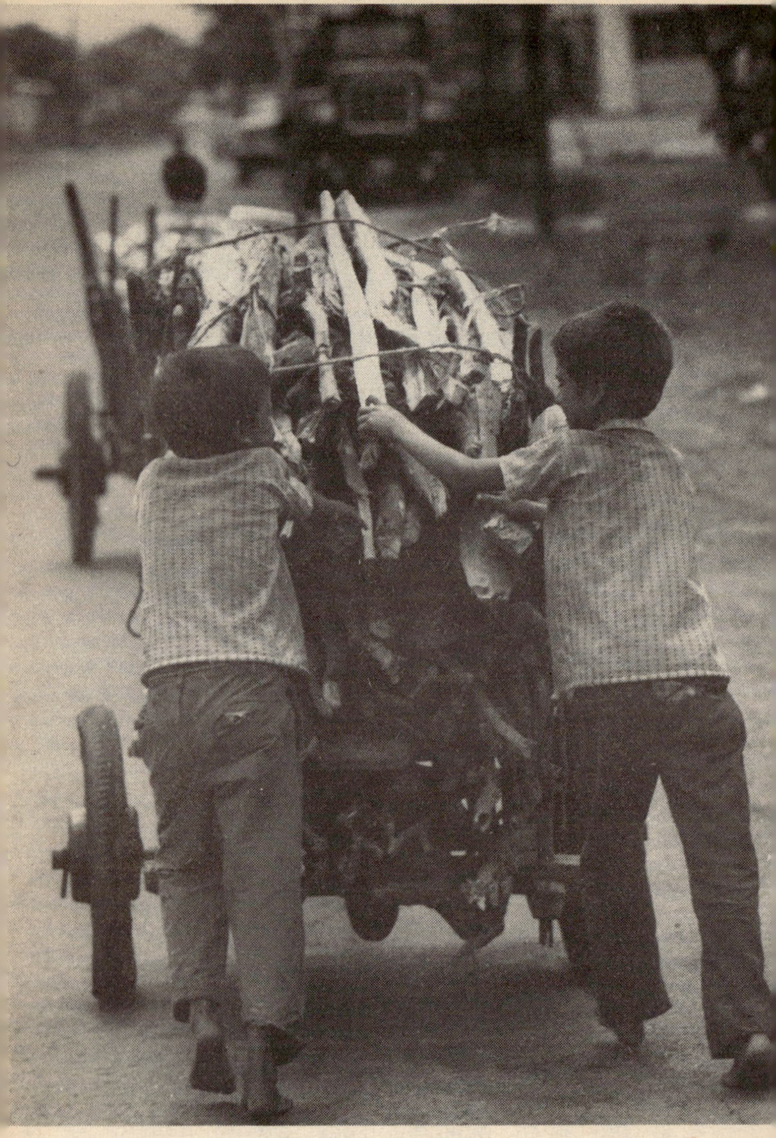

which could kill them, through accidents or industrial diseases, before they reach twenty. And it is about young people whose chances of education are denied them because they spend every hour of every day working to live, not to learn.

Usually, the pay the youngsters receive is abysmally low, almost always a fraction of the amount an adult would expect for the same work. On the tea plantations of India, for example, ten-year-olds can work a forty-hour week for half the adult wage. In other industries, children get no wages at all. Eleven-year-old Krishna, who works in the kitchen of an Indian hotel, is up at 5 o'clock every morning to start her exhausting, tedious job washing up and preparing vegetables. In return, she gets only her bed and meagre food rations. It is just marginally better than the street, which would be her only alternative.

Employers take advantage of young people's inability to defend themselves, physically and verbally, and they are sometimes beaten or made to work in difficult and unpleasant conditions. Often they are given dirty, monotonous or boring jobs which no adult would agree to do.

Dangerous conditions are another occupational hazard for the working child. Youngsters like Otami, whose story has been told earlier in this book, might spend the day in a factory without proper ventilation or lighting, or be forced to sit or stand in cramped conditions.

> *Work, work, work, that's all we ever do,*
> *This is unfair to me and it's unfair to you.*
> *Freedom of choice is one of our rights,*
> *But the cruelty in here has reached new heights.*

> *The selfish men treat me like an animal,*
> *This is not work, it's shameful.*
> *The conditions inhuman, the work is hard,*
> *And because of this from being a human I am barred.*
>
> Phillip Seddon, 14

Work stints the child's educational and psychological development. Cooped up in a sweatshop or isolated in a field all day, there is little to develop his or her communicative skills. And, since the jobs children do are almost always undemanding, they often grow up without much self-esteem.

How Many Children Work?

Putting a figure on the number of child workers in the world today is no easy task. One major problem is that most of them are "invisible", in illegal or "informal" jobs, and so are not included in official statistics. Many are unpaid family workers, like thirteen-year-old Meena, who spends her days cooking and doing housework so that both her parents can work on a Malaysian palm oil plantation. Others are domestic workers outside their own home, like one thirteen-year-old girl researchers found in Kenya, who received only a tiny wage and her board and lodging in return for caring for a ten-month-old child. She had to get up at 5 a.m. to clean the house, wash and iron clothes and cook breakfast for her mistress. At night, she slept in an airless storage room without even a window.

> *I think that the Government*
> *Of these places like Kenya, Brazil and Thailand*
> *Should put the employers of these children*
> *In prison or fine them ten thousand pounds.*
>
> James Rowbotham, 10

Guesstimates, however, put the figure as high as 150 million worldwide. The Anti-Slavery Society, which closely monitors the problem, believes the total to be well over 100 million. The International Labour Organization (ILO), meanwhile, suggests that 18 per cent of ten- to fourteen-year-olds in the developing world are economically active.

The biggest concentration of child workers is in Asia, where children make up at least a tenth of the entire work force. In the southern part of the continent more than 60 per cent of youngsters work, and the figure for India, boosted by child exploitation in the tea gardens of Assam, could be higher.

In some countries in Africa as many as 40 per cent of under-fifteens are believed to work, making up 17 per cent of all those employed. And in parts of Latin America, one in four children has a job.

But child labour is not confined to the poorer countries. Several million youngsters work in western Europe and North America. In Italy, as many as half a million under-fifteens are thought to be employed in industries including shoe- and lace-making, and on a seasonal basis harvesting crops such as grapes, tomatoes and olives.

In general the vast majority of child workers in the West are service staff – newspaper deliverers, waiters, petrol station attendants. Like other child labourers, they are almost always badly paid and often do jobs an adult would refuse.

Even in Britain as many as 1.8 million children work, according to a report published by the Anti-Slavery Society. Most of their jobs, it says, are badly paid – the Society's researchers found thirteen-year-olds doing farm work from 8 a.m. to 6 p.m. at weekends for payment of just 90 pence an hour. Another thirteen-year-old, a garage worker, received just 13 pence an hour for his labour. And an alarming number of the jobs may even be dangerous – one earlier study found that nearly a third of the working children they surveyed had suffered some accident or injury at work.

That report, based on a survey of 449 children in London, Cardiff, the West Midlands, Norfolk, Cambridgeshire and Glasgow, estimated that between 30 and 40 per cent of children aged 11–15 were at work in Britain. The 449 had 483 jobs between them, and the youngest child discovered working was a four-year-old girl who modelled clothes.

In theory, children with jobs in most parts of Britain should have a permit signed by both their parents and their headteacher. But the survey found that only a handful had these.

The children did a wide assortment of jobs; amongst them were porters, supermarket stockers, waiters, cleaners and clerical assistants. The most popular job, though, was delivering newspapers.

According to British law, no child under thirteen may work (except in some jobs such as modelling and acting). Older children are not to work before 7 a.m. or after 7 p.m., or for more than two hours on a Saturday and Sunday. They are not to work in dance halls, discos, slaughter houses or domestic kitchens.

There is absolutely no doubt that many youngsters are working outside the boundaries of what is legal in Britain at the present time.

Among the cases uncovered by the Anti-Slavery Society were those of many children, particularly in the 12–13 age group, whose schoolwork was suffering, and who could not do their homework properly because of their job. In the West Midlands, there were teenage girls whose leisure hours were almost entirely filled by helping their mothers do piecework – jobs such as trimming, packaging and finishing garments. In addition, most did housework, shopping and cooking.

But generally speaking, although child labour in Britain may be a more serious problem than it is usually considered to be, it pales into insignificance beside the enormity of the burden placed on youngsters in the developing countries.

There, children are to be found in virtually every industry, on the majority of plantations, and, increasingly, on every street corner. On the labour-intensive plantations of countries such as Kenya, Malaysia and Brazil, children are welcomed as workers because they are often quicker than adults. They are also cheaper, as they rarely receive more than a fraction of the adult wage.

Many industries recognize the usefulness of child labour. Youngsters are exceptionally efficient brickmakers, for example, and make an important contribution to the success of the Indian brick business. Most of the children who work in it belong to migrant families from rural areas who drift to the cities seeking work. They tend to be members of the lowest Hindu caste, and hence the least important social group. Work is seasonal, because the bricks must be made in the summer when they can be dried under the hot sun. Therefore pressure is intense to get the work done before the weather turns nasty: children and their parents frequently have to work through the night.

In other parts of the world, whole industries are run virtually entirely on child labour. The carpet-making industries of some North African countries are perhaps most notorious in this respect: five-year-olds working looms for up to twelve hours a day are not uncommon there.

They work and work and work all day.
And only receive minimum pay.
They find it hard to survive,
While we in Europe can easily thrive.
We send money but not our heart,
This is tearing the world apart.

Stephanie Bryceland, 12

Why Do Children Work?

When youngsters work in Britain it is usually to give them a bit of pocket money for evenings out or trips to the cinema. But elsewhere, a young person's wages can mean the difference between life and death for his family. Research indicates that children's pay makes up as much as 30 per cent of the family income in some parts of the Third World:

some teenagers are even the main wage earner. In Hyderabad, India, one thirteen-year-old factory tea girl's daily wage of 25 pence supported herself, her mother and four brothers and sisters. In Colombo, Sri Lanka, a fourteen-year-old brush salesboy told a researcher: "I have to do this work. I have a family to support. I have a younger brother who is smart in school. He is good at learning and I want to make him have a good education."

Elsewhere the story is much the same. Sarai of Bangalore, in India, lives with her mother in a shanty house, and spends her days sorting through rubbish and trying to sell anything of value she finds. "Mummy is too sick to work", she said when questioned about her life. "We live from what I can earn."

Or there is Raju, an eight-year-old who works as a domestic cleaner in a Calcutta household. For a punishing day of dusting, washing and water-fetching, Raju receives his meals as wages. Yet even these are not for him alone: he must save part of the food for his mother at home.

Poverty is the real cause of child labour in the developing countries. The more widespread the poverty, the higher the number of working youngsters. If a family does not have enough money to survive, it is forced to look at every possible way of increasing its income. Children, even those too young to walk and talk, have definite earning potential and, in desperate situations, must earn their keep.

Often children are set to work as young as three or four years old. They help around the home, fetching and carrying, or they do simple tasks such as preparing vegetables. The more household chores

Child Labour 95

the little ones do, the more time the older children and parents have to work in the fields or at the factory.

In some places, particularly on the large plantations, employers engineer the conditions to ensure that children do have to work. They keep the adult wage to a minimum to ensure that parents cannot earn enough for even basic needs. Or they may pay individuals on a piece rate, which they can only make into a living wage by using other family members to help. Occasionally, employers even hire whole families on a contract basis.

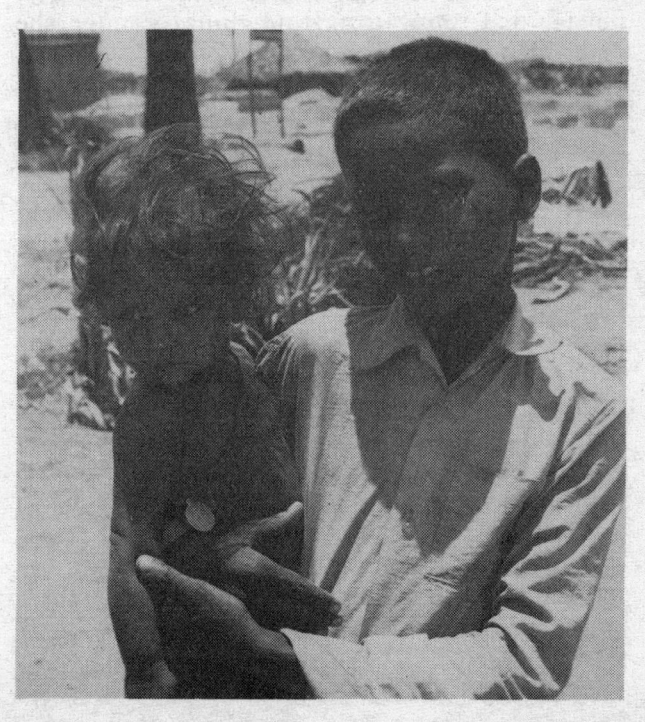

In times of hardship – when someone is ill, or when the woman of the house is pregnant – things are particularly difficult for the Third World family, and the children have to do more work than ever.

Proper welfare systems, with payments to top up the family income in times of need, would help keep children out of the work force. If parents received unemployment benefit when they were out of work, or if they could expect child benefits while bringing up a family, they might be able to afford not to send their children out to work. But not all countries are rich enough to provide such a safety net for their inhabitants, and children suffer as a result.

> *Is this the world we live in?*
> *Where the families in the Third World are torn apart.*
> *We sometimes accuse the government of having no heart,*
> *But we too are responsible for the things they miss.*
> *Because we do not want to sacrifice*
> *A small part of our everyday bliss.*
>
> Antonia Greenan, 12

General conditions in much of the world, then, contribute to a climate in which working children have become the norm. Employers do little to discourage it: they are only too pleased to have children working for them, for after all, they are much cheaper than adult employees.

They are also less trouble. Children do not get involved in trades unions or go on strike. But this also means that they have no rights of employment, and can be hired and fired at the employer's whim. In this respect, tragically, child labour creates a vicious circle: their continued employment prevents trade unionism, which might help reform the system, from getting a proper hold in the work place.

Children are often preferred as factory workers because of their size and agility. In the Indian tea plantations, for example, their soft, nimble hands do not bruise the leaves as adults' often do.

A final reason why child labour thrives in the developing world is that, quite simply, there are large numbers of children to fuel the market. The dramatic drop in infant mortality has meant that Africa, Asia and Latin America have more young people than ever before. In Pakistan, for example, infant mortality dropped from 160 per 1,000 in 1961 to 120 per 1,000 twenty years later. In Bangladesh, 46 per cent of the population are under fifteen. Most start work before the age of twelve.

Unfortunately, the population explosion did not coincide with a dramatic growth in employment opportunities. Instead, the lack of jobs hit the rural areas particularly hard, and meant country dwellers left home in their tens of thousands to try their luck in the big cities. Too late, they realized their mistake: there were no jobs for them. All they had done was to exchange one kind of poverty for another, and the new variety was much filthier and more extreme than the one they had known before – the poverty of the slums.

Every major Third World city has its slum quarter – as indeed do many cities in Europe. Sometimes, as with the Mathare Valley in Nairobi, it is only a short drive from the grand, air-conditioned hotels of the Westernized town centre. The contrast could not be more stark. Five minutes from the safe haven of the Hilton a scene of utter deprivation stretches as far as the eye can see. The stench is appalling, the flies are everywhere, toddlers play knee-deep in mud surrounded by pigs, goats and chickens.

It is not surprising, then, that many children decide anything would be better than life in these annexes of hell. Desperate, they make for the city streets, where they scrape whatever living they can from the pavements.

> *If I was that child*
> *I would be frightened.*
> *If I was that child*
> *I would be crying.*
> *If I was that child*
> *I would be cold.*
> *If I was that child*
> *I would be dying.*
> *Help that child, God.*

Aidan Turner, 8

What are the Risks for Child Workers?

Nine-year-old Shadab has never been to school. He works a twelve-hour day, six days a week, and has done so for the last three years. His job involves polishing bits of metal on a high-speed wheel in a New Delhi lock-making factory.

Shadab wears no protective clothing and could easily be maimed if the wheel mechanism snapped. The metal dust has turned his skin grey and stiffened his hair. His voice is hoarse, and he will probably develop throat disease in later life because of the cumulative effect of inhaling metal fragments. He is typical of child workers throughout the developing world in the appalling dangers he faces every day of his life.

At the forefront of these are the health risks. Like Shadab, many children who work are at risk from unprotected machinery. Ten-year-old Ramu, of Gangenhalli in India, lost four fingers from his right hand in a gory accident with a sugar cane crushing machine in the restaurant where he was employed as a washer-up. Another young worker, thirteen-year-old Shamsul Nizam, was lucky to escape with his life after he fell into an ice-crushing machine at a fish-packing factory in Malaysia. Friends pulled him to safety, but he lost his right arm in the accident.

But even the children who survive the perilous machines of their work places are unlikely to reach adulthood unscathed. Most do their jobs in environments thick with dust, pollutants, and carcinogens. On plantations, the air is usually full of toxic pesticides and other chemicals – often of brands which have been banned in the West. Jamilah, who started work on a Malaysian plantation at the age of eleven, died just before her eighteenth birthday from respiratory cancer caused by pesticides.

Many other youngsters working on plantations are worn down by the unpleasantness and discomfort of their work. Ronel Canar, aged twelve, is a sugar cane worker in the Philippines. His head is shaven so that he won't catch lice, and he has thin limbs and knobbly knees. He describes cutting cane as "torture". The stems have fine hairs along them which cause skin irritations. "And the heat is terrible. Sweat drips into your eyes and blinds you. There's no time for rest."

Factory workers are at risk from dangerous chemicals, too. Many of the ten thousand adolescents registered as employees in the Sao Paulo glass industry will develop cancers from the cleaning chemicals they have to use.

Many youngsters are also the victims of deliberate violence meted out by employers. Beatings, sexual abuse and even torture are not uncommon. Seven youngsters, all under twelve, who tried to run away from their jobs as carpet-weavers in Mirzapur, India, were punished by being strung upside down from a tree and branded with hot irons. And on a South African farm a thirteen-year-old child was horse-whipped to death for allegedly damaging grain sacks.

It is not surprising, then, that few children escape unscathed from their years of labour on the plantation or in the sweatshop. Even the luckiest are weak, thin and feeble by the time they reach their twentieth birthday, and many cannot hope to live much beyond the age of forty-five.

Given the horrific conditions they have to endure, it is hardly surprising that many working children suffer psychologically. You cannot take a person at the most formative stage of his life, subject him to appalling conditions and dangers, and then expect him to grow into a well-balanced individual. Typically, child workers tend to be withdrawn and introverted. Often they feel worthless and lack any kind of confidence.

People live and people die,
People kill, I don't know why.
I just don't know why,
I just think of myself as a flower crying out blood,
Or corn getting cut.

102   *Hidden Hands*

*I live in a faraway country, friends dying every
    day,
Every day.
I live in a world of make-believe,
I live in a world of fantasy,
Fantasy.*

*You people calling out for peace,
We people saying feed us please,
Feed us please,
So let you British help us dying now today,
Yes today.*

Cliff Cook, 12

Child Labour

Many, particularly children who live on the streets, are continually up against negative attitudes and a barrage of insults from those around them. In time, even the most buoyant become worn down and lose their self-esteem.

Children who have lived on the streets for a time also tend to develop an "instant" attitude to life. Because they exist from minute to minute, day to day, they are quite unused to any concept of the long term. They lose the ability to concentrate for any length of time. If they decide they want to learn to read, they expect to be able to do it in a day, and are unable to work beyond that period.

As well as the emotional toll of being separated from their parents, those working children who are alone lose even limited access to any support network, such as those run by churches and voluntary organizations, where they exist. They are isolated, and have no one to worry about them or account for them.

The problem is particularly worrying as street children are one of the fastest growing groups of child workers in the Third World. Some estimates put their number as high as 80 million. Every major city of the developing world now has its communities of youngsters who sleep, eat, work, give birth and die on the streets.

At least in part, they are another result of the growing shift from the rural areas to the cities. Many families who migrated to the shanty towns found that they just could not cope with all the mouths they had to feed. The older ones were frequently left to make their way alone. Others who live on the streets moved out after suffering violence at the hands of drunken fathers; yet more are orphans. Whatever their reason for being there, they have at least one common bond: none has anywhere else to go.

Some, desperate for cash, have turned to hazardous ways of moneymaking. Among these are the "dragons" of Mexico City – young fire-eaters who perform their trick at road junctions when the lights are at red, then collect the coins thrown at them from car windows. Their spectacular feat often earns them more cash than they would get from selling newspapers, but at a cost: many "dragons" suffer severe burns to their throats and mouths.

But the most brutal and violent life any child worker has must be that of a soldier. Twenty nations in the world are thought to have under-fifteens in their armies, among them Uganda and Iran. In Uganda many fifteen-year-olds joined up with Yoweri Museveni's resistance forces, and fought in the war that led to him becoming president in January 1986. There are still thought to be between two and three thousand child soldiers, known as *kadagos*, in the country. Many are being taught to fire guns they can scarcely lift.

Some young soldiers become sucked into the army after being "helpers" – carrying food and ammunition – for a time. They become absorbed in army life, which many undoubtedly enjoy very much. All too often it ends in tragedy, as it did for twelve-year-old Thaung Ohn, a member of the Karen National Liberatiorn Army in Burma. Thaung lost his leg two years ago when he trod on a mine.

Yesterday, Mr Wilberforce abolished slavery.
"There will be no more slaves", he said.
Today there will be more slaves than a hundred
*   years ago,*
Child labour among them.

Children are born to be educated,
Today in the Third World most are working,
At sixteen, when they should be starting,
They are forced into mandatory retirement.

Ryan Miner, 14

Children For Sale

Using children as workers has made them into a commodity in some countries. They are bought and even stolen, then sold to the highest bidder.

Thailand could be called a centre of the child trade, as Otami's story showed. The hub of the trade is Hua Lampong Railway Station in Bangkok, where representatives of job agencies and brokers hang around seeking out young newcomers to lure away with the promise of advance wages and somewhere to live. Once the youngsters receive their downpayment, however, they are tied to the employer and find themselves trapped in some unsavoury sweatshop where they are required to sew garments or assemble electrical goods from dawn till dusk.

Yet another group of child workers are those whose fate is sealed at birth. They are the offspring of bonded labourers, children who inherit their parents' burdens from the moment they take their first breath.

Bonded labour, which is particularly widespread in India and other parts of Asia, is recognized by the United Nations as a form of slavery. It happens when the head of a household, faced with absolute poverty, is forced to borrow money but has only his labour to offer in return. In effect, he sells himself to a master – and though he may work hard to pay off the debt, it seems to go on increasing as the 'interest' mounts up. Usually the bondsmen find it impossible to clear their debt, and their children, and even their grandchildren, pay for it with a lifetime of unpaid service.

Why should we be concerned about Child Labour?

On a purely humanitarian level, it is difficult NOT to be concerned about the suffering of millions of young people around the world. But there are less passionate considerations, too. For one thing, humanity is obviously failing to make good use of its best resources, its children. By misusing the early years of their lives, these youngsters are effectively being prevented from making the best of themselves in later life. Their futures are being stolen from them at the outset, and they are being denied any chance of development. For the world in general, meanwhile, a new generation of unhealthy, illiterate adults is growing up.

> *Will they be happy?*
> *Will they be sad?*
> *Help me God, please.*
> *I want to be with them.*
>
> Catherine Melis, 9

After proper food and shelter, the most serious thing many child workers are being denied is an education. For most, the possibility of attending a school is ruled out because classes are run at precisely the same time as they work – during the daytime. In any case, school fees, books and uniforms are too expensive for poor families, and in many countries education does not come free.

If the children were being taught some useful trade at work it might go some way towards compensating for their lack of formal schooling. But few receive any kind of training: child work is usually mechanical, meaningless and menial.

Sadly, many experts believe child labour is on the increase. The worsening economic situation in much of the Third World, caused amongst other things by the debt repayments demanded by Western nations, is at least part of the reason why. As long as countries have families living on the brink of survival, child labour will continue to be the only way to stave off starvation for many of them.

*People die and people cry
and people call out.
Feed us please, oh feed us please,
This world is falling out.*

Nicola Bacon, 13

The rise in the number of urban dwellers in the developing world also contributes to the concern for the future. Since 1945, the cities of Brazil, Colombia and Mexico have increased from about 30 per cent of the total population to 70 per cent. In the same period, Manila has increased fivefold and Bangkok sevenfold. By the year 2000, the world will have more urban than rural dwellers, and the number of street children is bound to increase as a result.

What can be done about Child Labour?

Clearly, something must be done. As we have seen, millions of children are being made to work in totally unacceptable conditions. They are denied their right to education, to family care and to a future.

Poverty is the root cause of the problem. In the developing countries, children do not work through their own or their parents' choice: they work because otherwise their families would starve. So it follows that child labour will only finally be abolished when the world is freed from the widespread and acute poverty which grips it at the moment.

Because of this, it is important to realize that policies which are not directly about child labour may nevertheless have an important role in helping to eliminate it. For example, money spent on rural development means that fewer villagers are forced to leave the countryside because of poverty. And that, in turn, means fewer children joining the ranks of street children in big cities.

In the same way, companies (particularly multinational corporations) which agree to pay better wages will help reduce child labour in the long term, because better-off employees will cease to be so dependent on their children's income.

But by far the most effective way of keeping children out of the labour market is to send them to school. Compulsory, full-time education has been the most effective way of eradicating child labour yet devised. In nineteenth-century Britain it was education acts, rather than anti-child labour legislation, which removed youngsters from the mines and workshops of the industrial revolution.

This has also been the pattern in the developing countries today. Many have been able to expand their education over the last twenty years – UNESCO figures show that the school enrolment ratio for children aged six to eleven in Africa more than doubled between 1960 and 1985, rising from 32 per cent to 66 per cent. Some nations, including Kenya, Tanzania and Sri Lanka, have achieved almost universal primary education; this means at least that the youngest children are no longer available for work. Other nations, though, still have much to achieve in the field of education, and therefore it is only realistic to presume that child labour will continue to be the norm for some time to come.

For, even if it were possible, it would not be desirable to order an immediate clampdown on child labour. Any such action would almost certainly increase the exploitation of youngsters still more, by forcing factory owners to hide their child workers away and treat them worse than ever. Far better for countries to aim at improving conditions for young people by limiting the number of hours they can work, and by ensuring they receive decent wages, have weekly rest days, annual holidays and medical care.

Countries with children working in particularly dangerous industries such as mining, glass making and the manufacture of fireworks, also need to draw up better safety regulations for factories, and to set up a better and more efficient system of inspecting them.

The majority of Third World countries already outlaw child labour but these laws are not yet effective. India, for example, bans hazardous employment for under-fifteens – yet it is one of the most notorious employers of children. In Sri Lanka, a country where five-year-old tea pickers are common, the legal minimum age for employment is fourteen. It is illegal to employ under-sixteens in South Africa – but black youngsters have to work to survive.

So, clearly, we have to be realistic. It would be neither possible nor desirable to expect all children to stop working overnight – if they did, most of them, and their families, would probably starve. The way forward must be a gradual one, and programmes to eliminate child work must be carefully geared so that they are relevant to their present lives. Street children, for example, are likely to be understandably resentful of suddenly being told what to do after they have become used to their independence. Also, they have no reason to trust adults – the ones they encounter are likely to be abusive, perhaps even violent, towards them.

It is not surprising, then, that the old way of

112   *Hidden Hands*

dealing with street children – rounding them up and putting them in "corrective institutions" – was not only harsh, but it also failed to do them any good. Most youngsters treated in this way went back to their old way of life as soon as they were released.

Street children, perhaps more than any other category of child worker, have to be handled carefully. From their point of view, the streets are a place where they can be independent, free from adult interference, their own bosses. Those who hope to help them will fail if they do anything to threaten that life style. Because of this, some of the most successful initiatives include strong elements of self-help and self-government, putting the onus on children to sort out their own chores and priorities.

Among the best of this type of project is the Boys'

Society of Sierra Leone, an organization set up in 1966 and supported by various non-governmental and religious agencies, including the Catholic charity Caritas. The Society runs two homes for street boys and an outreach programme which provides food, clothes and medicines for fifty to eighty boys. In the homes the boys do their own cooking, cleaning and laundry, and the Society pays the children's school fees so that they can get an education.

More ambitious is the government-funded Bosconia project in Bogota, founded in the early 1970s by Catholic priest Javier de Nicolo. Based on the philosophy that street children need respect and friendship, the project centres on El Patio, a protected yard where about a hundred youngsters go each day for a meal and to wash their clothes. Father de Nicolo and his helpers go out with food in the evenings, telling more street children about El Patio and inviting them along. Any drugs or weapons the youngsters own are left at the gate of El Patio and returned to the children as they leave.

Some of those who attend El Patio go on to stay at a house called La Liberia, where drugs are banned. There they get a taste of life away from the streets. If they decide they do not want to go back to their old jobs, the youngsters go through a special ceremony, which includes burning their street clothes. Many go on to do well at school, and some have even got into universities. On the opposite page, street boys are photographed at a rehabilitation centre in Colombia, where they learn arts and crafts. Page 115 shows street children from the well-named Beit Al Amar (House of Hope) in the Sudan, acquiring new skills at a technical school.

There are other projects, too, which provide youngsters with opportunities to break out of dead-end jobs and find better ways of supporting themselves. Among them is the UNICEF-sponsored technical training school in Khartoum, where working children take courses in carpentry, welding and electrical maintenance. Because the scheme has the backing of the city's business community, graduates go on to find good apprentice jobs.

As well as government, church and agency-backed schemes, there are those started by working youngsters themselves. SKI Courier (Street Kids International) is a bicycle courier service in Khartoum set up by twenty street children. They work in the mornings, and spend their afternoons in the SKI office learning to read, write and do maths.

Girls have often been ignored by those seeking to help child workers. In many cases they are simply included in projects designed for boys, rather than recognized as having special needs of their own. One programme which seeks to rectify this problem is in San Jose, Costa Rica. It offers temporary shelter and ante- and post-natal care to pregnant teenagers, as well as giving them chances for vocational training and job placements.

Other types of programmes are designed to prevent youngsters ever becoming sucked into boring, no-hope jobs. In rural areas, schemes are run to encourage youngsters to stay in the country and farm the land like the children on page 106. CAFOD supports a scheme in Kenya to make youngsters more aware of the importance of staying on the land, both for themselves and for their communities. They are encouraged to join discussion groups, and are later offered courses in agriculture, fish-farming and poultry-breeding.

Information-gathering is another important aspect of tackling the problems of child workers. In many countries little is known about the extent to which youngsters are exploited, and governments are not always very willing to divulge their statistics. So, before non-governmental agencies and the churches can formulate programmes, assessments of needs have to be made. Several information-gathering organizations exist in the Third World: among them is the CAFOD-funded Support Group for Child Workers in Asia, an organization based in Bangkok which collects data and publicizes it through a quarterly newsletter. The group also produces books, posters and other audio-visual materials to help raise the level of awareness of the plight of child workers, and tries to bring it to the attention of politicians and decision-makers.

Clearly, then, there are many worthwhile projects being funded by charities, churches and governments around the world which are improving conditions for child workers. Those who seek to help have begun to understand that they must look closely at the youngsters' lives, hopes, fears and frustrations, and must endure that whatever they do is both relevant and accessible for them. But there are nowhere near enough of these initiatives yet. The majority of child workers remain, tragically, isolated, uncared for and exploited. In a world racked by inequality, children remain the most unequal of all.

Bibliography

All Work and No Play – Child Labour Today (TUC Resource Book, 1985)

School Age Workers in Britain Today by Caroline Moorehead (Anti-Slavery Society (ASS), 1987)

Child Labour in Thailand by Sumanta Banerjee (ASS, 1980)

Child Labour in Morocco's Carpet Industry (ASS, 1978)

Child Labour in Italy by Marina Valcarenghi (ASS, 1981)

Child Labour in India by Sumanta Banerjee (ASS, 1979)

Child Labour : A Briefing Manual (International Labour Organization, 1986)

Exploitation of Working Children and Street Children (UNICEF, 1986)

The Hunger Crop : Poverty and the Sugar Industry by Belinda Coote (Oxfam, 1987)

Africa's Crisis and the Church in Britain (CAFOD/Catholic Truth Society, 1987)

In addition materials on child labour for use in classroom discussions can be obtained by writing to:

CAFOD, 2 Romero Close, Stockwell Road, London SW9

The Anti-Slavery Society, 180 Brixton Rd, London SW9

UNICEF, 55 Lincolns Inn Fields, London WC2

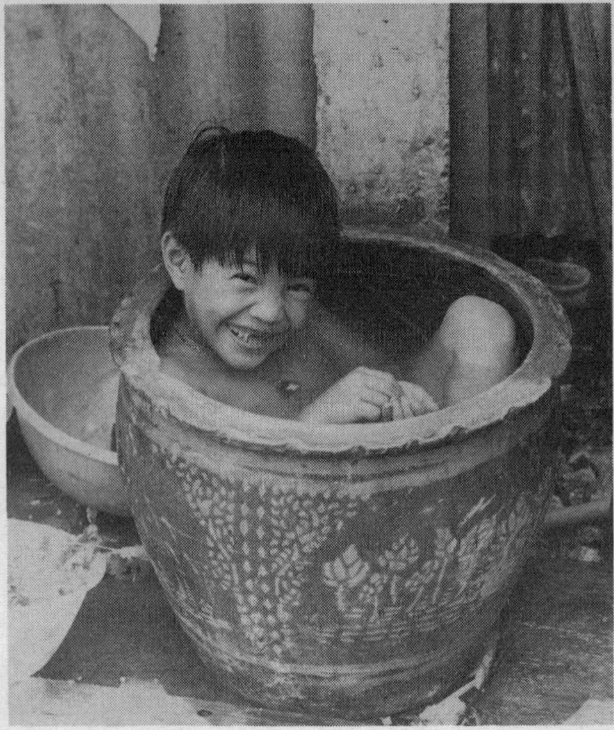

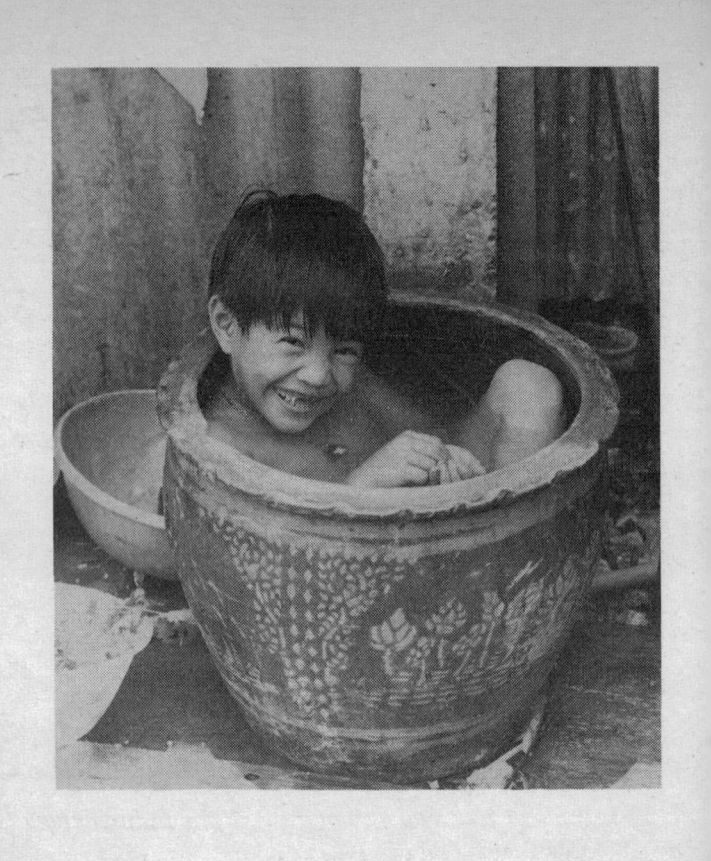

Publishers' Note

The stories of Kamau, Otami and Andrelina are fictitious, as are the children described in "Child Labour".

This book is not an indictment of any particular country – child labour, as can be seen, is common around the world, and is generally recognized for the evil it is. We are aware that members of governments – and individuals – in all the countries mentioned are involved in the effort to improve conditions for the children in whose hands our future lies.

The publishers